To

_____

From

_____

We dedicate this book to those who
introduced us to Jesus in the first place and
pressed upon us the importance of sitting at His feet.
May His life touch your heart as you read these
pages and experience the joy of His presence.

J.Y. & J.J.

To Jackie, Grandma's Princess.

C.B.

To my traveling companion, Patricia.

–O.A.

ZONDERKIDZ

The Princess Parables Daughters of the King, 90 Devotions
Copyright © 2017 by Zondervan
Written by Crystal Bowman
Illustrations © 2017 by Omar Aranda
Inspired by Jeanna Young and Jacqueline Johnson

Requests for information should be addressed to:

Zonderkidz, 3900 Sparks Drive SE, Grand Rapids, Michigan 49546

ISBN 978-0-310-75621-7

Illustrator: Omar Aranda
Design: Cindy Davis

Printed in China

23 24 25 /DSC/ 14 13 12 11 10 9 8 7 6 5 4 3

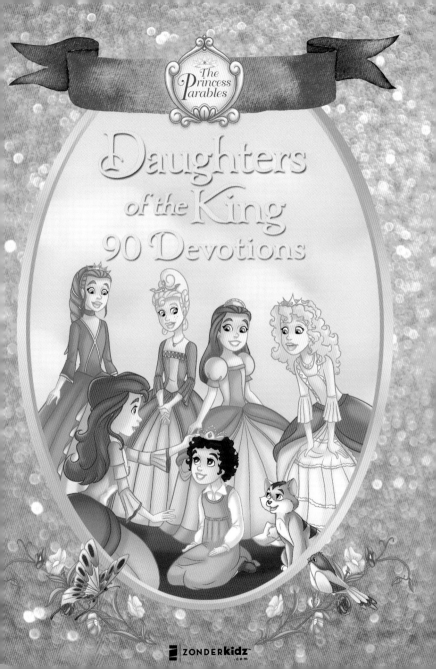

The Princess Parables

Daughters
of the King
90 Devotions

ZONDERkidz.com

MY FATHER THE KING

GOD'S GIFTS AND BLESSINGS

A SERVANT'S HEART

HAVE COURAGE

BE GIVING

BE JOYFUL

HAVE HOPE

GOD'S GRACE

FOREVER FAITH

See what amazing love the Father has given us!
Because of it, we are called children of God.
— 1 John 3:1

A Father's Love

Princess Charity and her sisters love their father. He is the king of the castle. But even though he is an important king, he cares about his daughters very much. He wants his daughters to be happy because he loves them. Did you know that God is your Father? He is your King and he loves you so much! God is more important than anyone in the whole world, but he cares about you. You are his daughter.

Princess Charity's Prayer

Thank you, Father,
for your love.
You are my King in
heaven above.

Live Like a Daughter of the King

God loves you from the top of your head to the tips of your toes. So put a smile on your face, stand on your tippy toes, and tell God you love him too!

*Lord, no one is like you. You are great.
You are mighty and powerful.*
—Jeremiah 10:6

The Greatest King

Princess Hope is happy that her father is the king. He is great and powerful because he is the king of his kingdom. But someday there will be another king in the land who will be as great and powerful as he is. With God it isn't like that. God is the only King of heaven and earth, and no other king will take his place. There is no other King like God. He is the greatest King of all.

Princess Hope's Prayer

**Lord, you are mighty
and powerful too.
Lord, there is no one
greater than you.**

Live Like a Daughter of the King

You might know about someone who is great or famous, but they probably don't know you. Think about this: God, who is the greatest King in the whole world, knows you! He knows your name and everything about you!

LORD, your love is as high as the heavens.
Your faithful love reaches up to the skies.
—Psalm 36:5

Sky High

Princess Hope and Princess Joy are looking at the great big sky high above the land and sea. They can see the clouds and birds, and the sky looks like it goes on forever. When God made the world, he made the sky so high that we cannot see where it ends. Only God, our Creator and King, could make the sky and put it up that high. The Bible tells us that God's love is as high as the sky. It is so high that it never ends.

Princess Joy's Prayer

Lord, your love is
higher than high.
It reaches way
beyond the sky.

Live Like a Daughter of the King

The next time you look into the sky, look way up high and think about God's love for you. Tell God "thank you" for loving you so much.

*LORD, the kingdom belongs to you. You are honored
as the one who rules over all.*
—1 Chronicles 29:11

Ruler Over All

Princess Charity likes riding her horse up to
Monument Hill. When she gets to the very top, she
looks out over the kingdom to see how far she can
see. Even though there are kings and rulers who
rule over the land, God is the one who really owns it
all. He is the King of kings and Ruler of rulers. The
mountains and hills, the flowers and trees, the earth
and sky belong to God because he made them all.

Princess Charity's Prayer

**Lord, you own
the sky and land.
You made it all
by your command.**

Live Like a Daughter of the King

What do you see when you look outside? Can you see birds and
trees? Maybe you see rocks or hills. Remember that God rules
over everything you see. Everything belongs to him, including you!

Your Father knows what you need
even before you ask him.
—Matthew 6:8

He Already Knows

When Princess Faith woke up, she had a surprise waiting for her. The king had breakfast prepared, and it was ready to eat. Her father knew that she would need some toast and tea before starting her fun-filled day.

Just like the king, God knows what we need. We can ask God for things like food and clothes, or maybe a new friend. But do you know what? God already knows what you need because he is your Father.

Princess Faith's Prayer

You know what I need,
day and night.
What you give me
is always right.

Live Like a Daughter of the King

God likes it when you talk to him. If there is something you need, you can tell him and he will listen. He will give you what you need when the time is right.

*How good and pleasant it is when God's
people live together in peace!*
—Psalm 133:1

Peaceful Daughters

The king likes watching the princesses have fun together on a beautiful day. They are his daughters and he loves each one. The king is happy when his daughters are kind to each other and enjoy being together. Everything seems better when the princesses get along.

God is pleased when his daughters get along too. It's hard to get along with everyone all the time. But we can ask God our Father to help us live at peace with our friends, family, and all the people in our lives.

Princess Hope's Prayer

**Father, you hear
the words I say.
Help me to live in
peace each day.**

Live Like a Daughter of the King

Think about the people in your family. Is it better to argue with them or live at peace with them? God wants you to be a peacemaker. That's what pleases him.

*God is able to do far more than we
could ever ask for or imagine.*
—Ephesians 3:20

So Much More

Princess Faith wanted to grow a flower garden.
She and her sisters planted flower seeds. They prayed
and worked hard as they waited for the flowers to
grow. Then one day, the garden was filled with more
flowers than Faith had hoped for. She and her sisters
were surprised to see so many beautiful flowers!

God can do much more than we imagine. Only
God can do such great things. He rules the world and
he makes flowers grow.

Princess Faith's Prayer

*Nothing is too
hard for you.
Lord, you are great
in all you do.*

Live Like a Daughter of the King

Sometimes life is hard. Every day is not a happy day. When
you are having a hard time, talk to God about it. Ask him to
help you. He can do more than you can imagine!

Children, obey your parents as believers in the Lord.
Obey them because it's the right thing to do.
—Ephesians 6:1

The Right Thing to Do

Sometimes the king tells his daughters, "It's time to listen!" He loves them very much and wants them to be safe. He gives them rules to obey because he wants to protect them from danger.

God wants his daughters to be safe too. He wants them to obey their parents and to obey him. He gives good rules in the Bible that will protect his daughters and keep them from harm. When daughters obey their parents, they are also obeying God. It's the right thing to do.

Princess Charity's Prayer

Help me, Lord,
to hear and obey.
I want to obey
you every day.

Live Like a Daughter of the King

Do you know why God wants you to obey his rules? It's because he loves you and he knows what is best for you. When you obey, it shows God that you love him too.

There are many rooms in my Father's house.
—John 14:2

A Beautiful House

The king lives in a big, golden castle with lots of fancy rooms. Princess Grace and her sisters can live there too because the king is their father. It's a beautiful home where they can eat and sleep and play.

The Bible tells us that God has a big, beautiful house in heaven. It has lots of fancy rooms, and all of his children can live there with him someday. God's home is more beautiful than any other house, even a royal castle.

Princess Grace's Prayer

Someday, Lord,
I know I'll see
the beautiful home
you have for me.

Live Like a Daughter of the King

Isn't it exciting to think that someday you will live in a place that's more beautiful than a castle? If you are a daughter of the King, he's making room for you!

Tell all people about the
wonderful things he has done.
—1 Chronicles 16:24

God Is Wonderful

Princess Grace likes to remind her sisters that they have a wonderful father. "He loves us and takes care of us," she says. "We don't have to worry because he gives us everything we need."

You have a wonderful Father too. God is your heavenly Father who loves you and cares for you. Do you enjoy playing in the world he made? Do you have food to eat and clothes to wear? Those are wonderful things! Remember to tell your friends and family about the wonderful things God does for you.

Princess Grace's Prayer

You are wonderful,
Lord, it's true!
I'll tell everyone
what you do.

Live Like a Daughter of the King

Before you go to bed tonight, think about something wonderful that God did for you today. Tell someone you know about that wonderful thing. Then say "thank you" to God for being so wonderful.

Every good gift and every
perfect gift is from above.
—James 1:17

Good Gifts

Princess Joy is having fun at her birthday party. Now it's time to open presents! But Joy has an idea. Instead of keeping the gifts for herself, she wants to give them to her friends so they can enjoy them.

God has many gifts that he wants to give you to enjoy. His gifts don't come in boxes with fancy ribbons. God's gifts are things like family and friends, singing birds, and pretty flowers. And the best gift of all is the gift of Jesus! God's gifts are always good.

Princess Joy's Prayer

Lord, your gifts
are from above.
Every gift is wrapped
in love.

Live Like a Daughter of the King

What are some of your favorite things? Do you have a pet or a favorite doll? Maybe you have a tree you like to climb. Those are gifts from God. Remember to thank God for his special gifts.

The LORD gives wisdom. Knowledge and understanding come from his mouth.
—*Proverbs 2:6*

Lots to Learn

Princess Hope is reading a book. She likes to learn new things. Reading makes her wise and helps her understand more about her father's kingdom.

Do you want to be wise and learn new things? When you read the Bible, God gives you wisdom. The words in the Bible help you understand how much God loves you. They help you know how to please God with the things you do and say. Wisdom, knowledge, and understanding are wonderful gifts God wants to give you.

Princess Hope's Prayer

*Please give me wisdom
and knowledge too.
Lord, these blessings
come from you.*

Live Like a Daughter of the King

The secret to being wise is to learn more about God. You can do that by reading a Bible storybook or books that teach you about God. Then you can live like a wise daughter of the King!

*And God is able to shower all
kinds of blessings on you.*
—2 Corinthians 9:8

Furry Blessings

Princess Grace likes to play with her soft and
furry kittens. She likes to feed them and take care
of them. God gives us many blessings to enjoy, and
animals are one of those blessings. Even if you don't
have a pet, you can enjoy the animals that live
around you. You can listen to birds singing and
ducks quacking. You can watch bunnies hopping
through the grass or squirrels chasing each other up
a tree. Tell God "thank you" for his blessings—even
the furry ones!

Princess Grace's Prayer

*Thank you for
animals all around,
high in the air, or
down on the ground.*

Live Like a Daughter of the King

Did you know that God put people in charge of animals? That's
why it's important to be kind to animals and care for them. Maybe
some day God can use you to help an animal that's lost or hurt.

35

Blessings are like crowns on the
heads of those who do right.
—Proverbs 10:6

Royal Treasures

Princess Joy and her sisters are looking at some treasures they found in a chest. Do you see the pretty crown? Crowns are for royal people. They are worn by kings and queens and princesses and princes.

The Bible tells us that God's blessings are like crowns. He gives blessings to people who love him and obey him. When we become part of God's family, we are like royalty. God's blessings are all around us, and they are special treasures.

Princess Joy's Prayer

Thank you for blessings you give to me, like treasures fit for royalty.

Live Like a Daughter of the King

God gives us more blessings than we can count. When you go to bed tonight count as many blessings as you can. Then tell God "thank you" for treating you like a princess.

*He gives those who are thirsty all the water they want. He gives
those who are hungry all the good food they can eat.*
—*Psalm 107:9*

As Much as You Want

Princess Charity is sitting by a stream enjoying a tasty lunch. The king always makes sure his daughters have plenty to eat and drink. He wants them to have food when they are hungry and water when they are thirsty.

The Bible talks about another kind of hunger and thirst. When we are thirsty to know God and hungry to learn more about him, God promises that he will fill us with his goodness. He will give us as much as we want!

Princess Charity's Prayer

*Lord, I'm hungry
and thirsty too.
Fill me with goodness
that comes from you.*

Live Like a Daughter of the King

Whenever you read the Bible or talk to God, it's like being filled with spiritual food. Just like you eat food every day, it's good to spend time with God every day too. The "food" God gives is always the best!

*I will bless anyone who trusts in me. I will do good
things for the person who depends on me.*
—Jeremiah 17:7

Depend on God

Princess Joy and Princess Hope are enjoying
a sunny day on the castle lawn. The flowers are in
bloom, and their furry friends have come to say hello.
The princesses are blessed to live in a lovely place.
They depend on the king to care for them and give
them what they need.

God, our King, wants his daughters to depend on
him. When we trust in him, he will bless us with good
things like sunny days and flowers and maybe some
furry friends!

Princess Hope's Prayer

*Lord, I depend
on you today.
Help me to trust you
in every way.*

Live Like a Daughter of the King

Do you know what happens when you depend on God? The Holy
Spirit gives you the gift of peace. Peace is the opposite of worry.
It's another one of God's good gifts!

*God so loved the world that he gave his one and only Son.
Anyone who believes in him will not die but will have eternal life.*
—John 3:16

The Greatest Gift

Princess Grace and her sisters are getting ready
for the Easter celebration. It's a time when everyone
in the kingdom celebrates Jesus' resurrection. Jesus
is God's Son who was born as a baby. As a man, he
healed people and did many miracles. Then Jesus
died on a cross to take the punishment for our sins.
But Jesus came alive again, and that's what Easter is
all about! Everyone who believes in Jesus becomes
a child of God. And someday they can live in heaven
forever. Jesus is God's greatest gift!

Princess Grace's Prayer

*Thank you, Jesus,
for dying for me,
so I can live eternally.*

Live Like a Daughter of the King

Can you believe God loves you so much that he sent Jesus to die
for your sins? You can be a daughter of the King by believing in
Jesus. There is no greater gift!

As his children, we will receive all that he has for us.
We will share what Christ receives.
—Romans 8:17

Precious Jewels

Princess Hope can't wait to see what's inside the fancy jewelry box. There might be some sparkly rings or a silver locket. Hope knows that she and her sisters can share the jewels because the jewels belong to their father.

God's blessings are like precious jewels that he gives to his children who love Jesus. If you are a daughter of the King then you can share in God's special blessings. We can have some of those blessings now, and someday we will receive many more in heaven.

Princess Hope's Prayer

Thank you for the blessings you share with all your children everywhere.

Live Like a Daughter of the King

God's gifts and blessings are for you! His love, his promises, his wisdom, and his care are blessings you can enjoy every day. You don't have to wait!

*But the fruit the Holy Spirit produces is love, joy
and peace. It is being patient, kind and good.*
—*Galatians 5:22*

Patience Please

Princess Faith wants to grow flowers, but things
keep happening to them. She had so many, and now
there is only one. But do you know what? Faith is
patient and doesn't give up. Soon she will have the
most beautiful flower garden in the kingdom again!

Patience is a gift from the Holy Spirit to God's
children. The next time things don't go just right, or
you have to wait for something you need, ask God to
give you patience.

Princess Faith's Prayer

*Lord, please give me
patience today,
no matter what may
come my way.*

Live Like a Daughter of the King

Is there something you are waiting for right now? Are you
waiting for a new tooth to poke through? Maybe you're waiting
for a new brother or sister. It's hard to be patient, but God will
help if you ask him.

Blessed is the person who obeys the law of the LORD.
—Psalm 1:1

Obey and Be Blessed

Princess Joy and Princess Charity are happy because the king gave them a treat. The king loves them no matter what, but he is pleased when his daughters obey him and do what's right.

The Bible tells us that God's children are blessed when they obey him. God loves us no matter what, but he is pleased when we do what is right. God blesses his children with good things. Do you want to be happy and blessed? Then ask God to help you please him.

Princess Joy's Prayer

*Thank you, Lord,
that I am blessed.
Pleasing you is
always best.*

Live Like a Daughter of the King

Do you find that it's hard to obey sometimes? God knows it's hard, but he will help you if you ask him. God loves you so much. He wants to help you and bless you!

Serve one another in love.
—Galatians 5:13

Serve with Love

Princess Joy loves to have tea parties. She is pouring tea for Princess Grace and her bunny with floppy ears. Pretty soon she will wash the dishes and put them away. Princess Joy likes to serve her sisters and friends because she loves them.

When we love our friends and the people in our family, we want to do good things for them. Serving others is a way to show our love. Serving others shows God that we love him too.

Princess Joy's Prayer

Lord, I want a loving heart, so I can serve and do my part.

Live Like a Daughter of the King

No matter how old you are, you can serve others. You can help your mom fold clothes and put them away. You can help a friend find her missing pet. Whenever you serve, do it with love.

Don't hold back good from those who are worthy of it.
Don't hold it back when you can help.
—Proverbs 3:27

You Can Help

Princess Charity is worried about a boy who is hurt. She is hoping someone will help him. But then she decides to help him herself.

There are many ways you can help others and do good things. If your friend is hurt on the playground, you can see if she needs you to find a grown up. If you have brothers or sisters, you can help them make their beds or look for their shoes. God is pleased when we care about others and help them.

Princess Charity's Prayer

Help me to care the
way I should.
I want to help and
do what's good.

Live Like a Daughter of the King

When you wake up in the morning, ask God to show you how you can help someone. Helping and serving others will make you feel good inside!

Anyone who serves me must follow me.
—John 12:26

Follow Jesus

Princess Faith is excited to go outdoors and work in the royal flower garden. Her sisters are close behind her. They are going to work beside her.

If you are a daughter of the King, then you can follow Jesus. You can learn about him from the Bible and love people the way that he did. Being kind and showing respect to others is a way to serve and follow Jesus. When you follow Jesus, others will want to follow him too.

Princess Faith's Prayer

Jesus, I want to follow you and show your love in all I do.

Live Like a Daughter of the King

Jesus had many followers when he lived on earth. He still has followers today. If you love Jesus and care about others, you can be a daughter of the King and a follower of Jesus.

None of you should look out just for your own good.
Each of you should also look out for the good of others.
—Philippians 2:4

Celebrate with Others

It is Princess Joy's birthday, and her sisters are planning a big party for her. Princess Faith wants to be sure the cupcakes are just right. The other sisters are helping too. They want Joy's birthday party to be very special.

It's fun to be the birthday princess and have everyone celebrate your special day. But it's also fun to celebrate for someone else. When you work hard to make someone extra happy, you will feel happy too!

Princess Faith's Prayer

Thank you that
I can celebrate
so others can feel
happy and great.

Live Like a Daughter of the King

Do you want to make someone else feel special? Make a fancy card with glitter and ribbon and give it to your mom or sister or friend. Be sure to write I LOVE YOU on the card!

But as for me and my family,
we will serve the LORD.
—Joshua 24:15

God and Family

Ever since the princesses were little girls, their father taught them about God and how much God loves them. Princess Grace and her sisters are happy they can serve God and show his love to the people in their kingdom.

Whether your family is big or small, you can serve God too. You can read Bible stories and pray together. You can be kind to your neighbors and share God's love with them. And someday, you can teach your children to serve the Lord too.

Princess Grace's Prayer

Help my family to serve only you, and share your love in all we do.

Live Like a Daughter of the King

Think of some ways you can help your family serve God. Can you say a prayer at breakfast? Can you share your favorite Bible story? Maybe you can invite a neighbor to church. It's always good to serve God with your family!

Serve him faithfully. Do it with all your heart.
Think about the great things he has done for you.
— 1 Samuel 12:24

With All Your Heart

Princess Charity likes to care for Daisy and clean the stable. She doesn't mind if the job is messy. She works with all her heart because she loves Daisy so much.

We serve God because we love him. You might not have to clean a messy stable, but if you love God with your whole heart, then you will want to serve him by showing kindness to others. God has given you so many blessings that serving him is a way to say "thank you."

Princess Charity's Prayer

Lord, you've done so much for me, I want to serve you faithfully.

Live Like a Daughter of the King

What are some blessings that God has given you because he loves you? How can you show God you are thankful for his blessings?

Work as serving the Lord and not as serving people.
—*Ephesians 6:7*

Happy Workers

Princess Faith and her sisters like to have fancy parties and outdoor adventures. They like to play with their pets and read good stories. But sometimes they have work to do. Even though they would rather be playing, they don't mind working when they remember they are working for the king.

Doing your chores or helping in the yard can be hard work. But the Bible reminds us that when we work and use our talents, we are serving God. When we remember that, we will work with a smile on our face.

Princess Faith's Prayer

When I need to work awhile, help me to wear a happy smile.

Live Like a Daughter of the King

What are some blessings that God has given you because he loves you? How can you show God you are thankful for his blessings?

May all kings bow down to him. May all nations serve him.
—Psalm 72:11

Serve the King

The king and his princess daughters are politely greeting a knight who came to help them prepare for the kingdom's Easter celebration. The king has many people who help him and do things he needs them to do.

Kings like the princesses' father are very important, but even kings and rulers serve God. God's kingdom includes kings and queens, moms and dads, grandpas and grandmas, teenagers and children. Everyone who loves God is part of his family. And we are all his servants.

Princess Hope's Prayer

You are King over all the land.
Help me serve you the best that I can.

Live Like a Daughter of the King

No matter how you pray, God loves to hear your prayers. But when you bow your head, it shows honor and respect for God. The next time you pray, bow your head to show God that you serve him.

Let us not become tired of doing good. At the right time we will gather a crop if we don't give up.
—Galatians 6:9

Don't Give Up

Princess Grace and Princess Hope are excited to see the pretty flower garden in the castle courtyard. They worked hard to help Faith grow the flowers she dreamed of having. They were happy they did not give up!

Did you ever have to work hard at something? It's easy to give up when things get hard. But when it comes to doing good things and serving others, it's important not to give up. You can ask God to help you. He will give you strength to keep going.

Princess Grace's Prayer

Lord, give me strength to do my best. I know that I'll be happy and blessed.

Live Like a Daughter of the King

Doing your homework and chores can be hard. Even making friends can be hard. But if you don't give up, you will see that working hard can have a happy ending.

Your Father will reward you, because he sees what you do secretly.
—*Matthew 6:4*

A Good Reward

The king gave his daughters special gifts because they helped a little girl in the kingdom. Princess Grace and Princess Hope are holding their pretty baskets. They are happy with their father's gift.

Did you know that God sees the good things you do, even if no one else sees? He is pleased when you show love and kindness to others. And someday, when you see God in heaven, he will reward you for all the good things you've done.

Princess Grace's Prayer

I just want to serve you, Lord, and someday have a great reward.

Live Like a Daughter of the King

Did you ever get a reward for something you've done? Sometimes your good deed might not be noticed by others. When that happens, just remember that God sees everything, and he is pleased with you.

Even though I walk through the darkest valley,
I will not be afraid. You are with me.
—Psalm 23:4

God Is with You

Princess Hope and her sisters are in the royal wagon. The sky behind them is looking dark and scary. A storm is coming. The princesses know God is with them. They can ask him to keep them safe until the storm is over.

Thunderstorms can be scary, but other things can seem scary too. No matter what makes you afraid, remember that God is always with you. You can ask him to keep you safe until you are no longer afraid.

Princess Hope's Prayer

Thank you, Lord,
that you are near.
I'll be strong and
will not fear.

Live Like a Daughter of the King

Everyone is scared sometimes—even grown-ups. When scary things happen, remember you are not alone. God is right there and he wants you to talk to him.

He gives strength to those who are tired.
He gives power to those who are weak.
—Isaiah 40:29

So Tired

Princess Grace is so tired! She looked all through the kingdom and cannot find her kitten, Poppy. She is very worried and doesn't know what to do.

Worrying about our problems can make us feel tired and weak. Maybe you know someone who is sick. Maybe one of your friends is moving away. God doesn't want you to worry. He wants you to trust him to take care of things. When you ask God to help you, his power helps you feel strong instead of weak.

Princess Grace's Prayer

Lord, when problems come along, your love and power make me strong.

Live Like a Daughter of the King

Is there something you are worried about? Worrying can make you feel tired and can keep you from doing other things. Let God handle your worries and ask him to help you stay strong.

I keep my eyes always on the Lord. He is at my
right hand. So I will always be secure.
—*Psalm 16:8*

In His Arms

Princess Faith is holding Buttercup so she doesn't get away. She wants Buttercup to be safe and secure in her arms in case there is danger ahead.

God wants us to keep our eyes on him and stay close to him. We can do that by reading the Bible and praying to him. Being close to God will make you feel safe and secure. He will be there to help you in times of trouble. When you keep your eyes on God, it's like being in his arms.

Princess Faith's Prayer

Help me to keep
my eyes on you,
so I'll be safe
in all I do.

Live Like a Daughter of the King

You can keep your eyes on God by spending time with him every day. You talk to him when you pray, and you read his words in the Bible. God already knows you, and he wants you to know him too.

LORD, you are the one who gives us strength.
You are the one who keeps us safe.
—Isaiah 12:2

Be Safe

The princesses were riding in their wagon when it started to rain. They are trying to stay dry. Princess Joy is saying a prayer for God to keep them safe. She knows praying is always the best thing to do!

No matter if it's raining or sunny, there will be times when you need God to give you some extra protection. Remember that you can pray to God wherever you are. You can ask him to watch over you and keep you safe any time.

Princess Joy's Prayer

Keep me safe and
in your care.
I know you're with
me everywhere.

Live Like a Daughter of the King

Asking God to keep you safe is a prayer you can say every day. God never gets tired of your prayers. He cares about you and loves you very much.

God gave us his Spirit. And the Spirit doesn't make us weak and fearful. Instead, the Spirit gives us power and love.
—2 Timothy 1:7

Spirit Power

Princess Charity is ready to jump on Daisy and ride her back to the palace. She needs to help someone who is hurt, and she has no time to lose. Charity knows the Holy Spirit will give her the courage she needs right now.

When you are a daughter of the King, the Holy Spirit gives you courage to do what God wants you to do. So don't be afraid! You can ask God to give you the Spirit's courage anytime and anywhere.

Princess Charity's Prayer

Lord, you hear me when I pray. I need your love and courage today.

Live Like a Daughter of the King

Did you know the feeling of fear is not from God? God doesn't want you to be afraid. He wants you to feel his power and love instead of fear. All you need to do is ask him!

*Be strong, all you who put your hope in
the LORD. Never give up.*
—Psalm 31:24

Never Quit!

Princess Grace and her sisters are searching for
their lost kitten in the woods. They see scary shadows
and they hear animals howling. But they are not going
to quit until they find Poppy. They know God will give
them courage to keep searching.

Sometimes life is hard. Sometimes things are scary.
Sometimes you might feel like quitting. But with God's
help, you can have the courage to keep doing what you
need to do. With God's help, you never have to quit.

Princess Grace's Prayer

*Lord, please keep
me going strong.
I need your help
all day long.*

Live Like a Daughter of the King

Do you have something in your life that is hard right now?
If so, ask God to help you. Let his love and strength give you
courage to keep going. You can always count on him!

Turn all your worries over to him. He cares about you.
—1 Peter 5:7

No More Worries

Princess Faith is leading her sisters through a dark tunnel. Her sisters are worried about the creepy noises and spider webs. But Princess Grace is not worried. She knows the tunnel leads to a beautiful courtyard.

It's easy to worry about things we don't understand. It's easy to worry about things that frighten us. But God doesn't want you to worry. He cares about you and wants you to give your worries to him. He wants you to talk to him and trust him.

Princess Faith's Prayer

When things are
hard to understand,
I'll put my worries
in your hand.

Live Like a Daughter of the King

When you say your prayers tonight, talk to God about the things that worry you. Tell him you are giving your worries to him. You might even sleep better!

*They aren't afraid when bad news comes. They stand
firm because they trust in the L*ORD.
—Psalm 112:7

Bad News

Princess Charity and her sisters are getting some
bad news. The friends they invited to Princess Joy's
birthday party are not going to come. But instead of
being afraid of Joy's birthday being ruined, Charity is
trusting God that everything will work out.

It's not fun to get bad news! But when you trust in
God, you can also trust that he can make everything
okay. If things don't get better right away, just keep
trusting and don't be afraid. Knowing that God is in
control is good news!

Princess Charity's Prayer

Lord, when bad
news comes my way,
I know that things
will be okay.

Live Like a Daughter of the King

Have you had some bad news lately? God doesn't want you to
worry or be afraid. Even though it might be hard, he wants you to
trust him. Just keep telling him how you feel, and he will listen.

God is our place of safety. He gives us strength.
He is always there to help us in times of trouble.
—Psalm 46:1

A Safe Place

Poppy is being brave. She is waiting in a safe place until Princess Grace finds her. Poppy will soon be in the arms of Princess Grace, who will carry her back home.

The Bible says that God is our place of safety. We can talk to God about anything that makes us feel worried or afraid. Whenever we talk to God, he listens. Whenever we have troubles, God is there waiting to help us. If you need a place of safety, just talk to God!

Princess Grace's Prayer

God, you are there,
waiting for me.
Being with you is
a safe place to be.

Live Like a Daughter of the King

Do you talk to your parents or a friend when you have problems? It's good to talk to people you trust, but God wants you to talk to him too. Being close to God will make you feel safe.

Be strong and brave. Do not be afraid. Do not lose hope.
I am the LORD your God. I will be with you everywhere you go.
—Joshua 1:9

Brave and Fearless

Princess Charity loves riding Daisy over the
hills and through the forest. She loves exploring the
kingdom and is always looking for exciting adventures.
Charity is brave and fearless. She knows God promises
to be with her wherever she goes.

God is always with you too—at home, at school,
and at the park. No matter where you go, God is right
there with you. That's why he doesn't want you to be
afraid. He wants you to believe his promise. He wants
you to be brave and fearless!

Princess Charity's Prayer

*I can be brave
because I know
you are with me
wherever I go.*

Live Like a Daughter of the King

Isn't it great to know that God is with you no matter where you go?
Your parents and friends can't always be with you, but God can.
He promises he will never leave you.

Give, and it will be given to you.
—Luke 6:38

Happy Giving

Princess Grace and her sisters are taking care of a little girl. She is sad because she wants her mommy. Grace has a good idea. She takes the tiara from her head and puts it on the little girl's head. Now the little girl is smiling. Grace is smiling too.

When we give a gift to someone else, we get a happy feeling inside. And the more we give, the happier we get! God is pleased when you give to others, and you will be pleased too!

Princess Grace's Prayer

Lord, my smile is big and wide! Giving makes me happy inside.

Live Like a Daughter of the King

It's fun to look for ways that you can give to others. Ask God to show you how you can give to someone today or tomorrow.

Share with the Lord's people who are in need.
Welcome others into your homes.
—Romans 12:13

Come on In!

Princess Joy is welcoming lots of children from the kingdom to her home. She wants them to come to her birthday party. They are not children who live in fancy homes or castles. Joy just wants to share her special day with them.

God wants us to share what we have with others. He wants us to invite others into our homes. It doesn't matter what kind of house or apartment you live in. When you invite someone to your home, you can share God's love with them.

Princess Joy's Prayer

Lord, I want to give and share to show how much I truly care.

Live Like a Daughter of the King

Is there someone in your neighborhood you can invite to a party or for dinner? Talk to your parents about it, then ask God to show you someone you can welcome into your home.

Each of you must bring a gift. Give to the LORD your God, just as he has given to you.
—Deuteronomy 16:17

Giving to God

It's almost time for the kingdom's Easter celebration. The king is telling Princess Charity that it's their turn to bring the gifts, the cross, and decorations. The kingdom celebrates Easter to remember the gift of salvation that Jesus gives.

When we remember the gift of Jesus, we can give gifts to show him how thankful we are. We can bring our money to church or give money and gifts to people who need them. There are many ways you can give back to God for giving us his Son.

Princess Charity's Prayer

Thank you, Father, for your Son, the greatest gift to everyone.

Live Like a Daughter of the King

When you say your prayers tonight, remember to thank God for the gift of Jesus. What is something you can give to show God you love him?

Command the rich to do what is good. Tell them to be rich in doing good things. They must give freely. They must be willing to share.
—1 Timothy 6:18

Giving and Sharing

Princess Grace and her sisters have many nice things. They wear pretty dresses and live in a castle. But their father reminds them to be kind and share with others. So Grace is giving her sisters a chance to play with her kittens. They will have fun playing together.

God is pleased when we share with our friends and people in our family. We can also share with people who need extra food or clothes. God gives us so many blessings, it's good to share them with others.

Princess Grace's Prayer

Sharing with others
is always good.
Help me to share
the way I should.

Live Like a Daughter of the King

When you say your prayers tonight, ask God to help you think of something you can share with someone else. You might be able to share with someone in your own family!

Those who give freely will be blessed. That's because they share their food with those who are poor.
—Proverbs 22:9

Let's Eat

Princess Joy is making a wish and blowing out her birthday candles. She is sharing her birthday dinner with boys and girls from all over the kingdom. They can't wait to enjoy the tasty food and delicious birthday cake!

Did you know some children are hungry because they don't get enough food to eat? Many cities and churches have places where you can bring food to help feed hungry people. God wants us to share with others, and when we do, we will be blessed.

Princess Joy's Prayer

Help me to share the very best. Lord, I know that I'll be blessed.

Live Like a Daughter of the King

Ask your parents if they can help you find a food pantry near your home. Maybe you can use your allowance to buy some food to help feed hungry people.

Each of you should give what you have decided in your heart to give. You shouldn't give if you don't want to. . . God loves a cheerful giver.
—2 Corinthians 9:7

Excited to Give

Princess Hope and her sisters are shaking their piggy banks to see how much money they have. They have decided to use their own money to buy a special treasure that was lost. They are happy and excited to give whatever they need to give.

That's how God wants us to give too. He doesn't want us to give because we have to. He wants us to give because we want to. God loves it when we give with joy in our hearts!

Princess Hope's Prayer

I want to give with joy in my heart, so I can bless others and do my part.

Live Like a Daughter of the King

It can be really fun to give a gift to someone else. Think of something you can give that makes you excited and happy to give. That's the kind of giving God loves.

*Give, and it will be given to you. A good amount
will be poured into your lap.*
—Luke 6:38

Give and Be Blessed

Princess Grace is enjoying her furry kittens. She gave them lots of love and attention when she found them. Now she cares for them every day. It's no surprise that Grace's kittens love her as much as she loves them!

The Bible tells us that when we give love and kindness to others, God will bless us. And the more we give to others, the more blessings God will give. God loves it when you give love and kindness to your friends—even your furry ones.

Princess Grace's Prayer

*Lord, when I give,
you give back to me.
Help me to always
give happily.*

Live Like a Daughter of the King

Can you think of a time when you were blessed because you were kind and giving to someone? Ask God to help you be kind and giving to someone this week. Then watch and see how God blesses you.

*Dear friends, let us love one another,
because love comes from God.*
— 1 John 4:7

A Big Hug

Princess Charity is giving Daisy a big hug. Giving someone a hug is a way to show you love them. You don't always have to give presents that cost money. A hug is a good gift too. Hugs make people feel loved. You can give a hug to your mom or dad. Grandpas and grandmas like hugs too. Even brothers and sisters need a hug. God wants us to show our love for others. And the best thing about hugs is they are free and easy to give!

Princess Charity's Prayer

*Help me to love
my family and friends.
Give me your love
that never ends.*

Live Like a Daughter of the King

Is there someone in your family who needs a hug today? You can make that person feel loved just by giving them a hug—and they will probably hug you back!

Kind words are like honey. They are sweet to the
spirit and bring healing to the body.
—Proverbs 16:24

The Gift of Words

Princess Charity helped a young boy even though she didn't know who he was. The boy's father is thanking Charity and speaking kindly to her. Princess Charity didn't want a reward, but the father's kind words are making her feel good inside.

Kind words are like a gift you can give to others. When you thank your mom for making your dinner, or tell your sister she is a good helper, it makes them happy. Words don't need to be wrapped in paper, they just need to be said.

Princess Charity's Prayer

> Help me to speak
> words that are kind,
> gifts that come from
> my heart and mind.

Live Like a Daughter of the King

As you go through your day, see how many times you can give the gift of kind words to someone else. The people who receive your gift will be very happy.

Give thanks to the Lord, because he is good.
His faithful love continues forever.
—Psalm 107:1

Give Thanks

Princess Faith is enjoying the fragrance of a pretty flower. She is thankful God creates many beautiful things. She will remember to thank God when she says her bedtime prayers.

Saying "thank you" to God for his blessings is like giving him a gift. He loves to hear us say "thank you." You can thank God for your family and friends. You can thank him for food and pets. You can even thank him for sunshine and rainbows! Giving thanks to God is a gift you can give every day!

Princess Faith's Prayer

Lord, I give my thanks to you, for you are great in all you do.

Live Like a Daughter of the King

Think of three things that you are thankful for. When you say your prayers tonight, tell God "thank you" for each one.

How you made me is amazing and wonderful.
I praise you for that.
—Psalm 139:14

You Are Special

Princess Charity is joyful because she knows God made her to be very special. She is brave and adventurous and full of energy. Each of her sisters is special too, because God made them different from each other.

Every person God creates is special. No two people are alike. God made you to have your own personality. He decided what color your hair and eyes should be. Besides creating you, God loves you—and that should put a big smile on your pretty face!

Princess Charity's Prayer

You made me special,
inside and out.
I want to sing and
dance and shout.

Live Like a Daughter of the King

There is no one else like you in the whole world! Think of ways that you are different from your friends or someone in your family. Thank God for making you special.

You young people, be happy while you are still young.
Let your heart be joyful while you are still strong.
—Ecclesiastes 11:9

Have Fun

Princess Grace is having fun playing outdoors with her sisters and their father. They are happy they can run and laugh and play games together.

Children have more time to play than grown-ups do. It's important to enjoy healthy activities while you are young. God made your body to do many different things. Maybe you enjoy running or climbing. If you can color or draw, those are good things too. You can keep your body and mind strong by doing the things you enjoy.

Princess Grace's Prayer

Thank you, Lord, for times of fun when I can play and laugh and run.

Live Like a Daughter of the King

What do you enjoy doing the most? God wants you to enjoy your life and do the things he created you to do. What is something fun you can do today?

Weeping can stay for the night.
But joy comes in the morning.
—Psalm 30:5

A Good Morning

Princess Joy is happy this morning because Rosebud is ready to play. No matter what happened the night before, waking up to a puppy is a good way to start the day!

Everyone has sad days, and sometimes life can be hard. But God makes each new day for you to enjoy. If you go to bed feeling sad, you can ask God to help you feel better in the morning. If you don't have a puppy to wake you up, you can look outside and smile at the birds.

Princess Joy's Prayer

Thank you, Lord,
for a day that's new.
I want to give my
praise to you.

Live Like a Daughter of the King

Talking to God is the best thing to do if you are sad. You can ask him to take away your sadness and fill your heart with joy. And always remember how much God loves you.

Worship the LORD with gladness.
Come to him with songs of joy.
—Psalm 100:2

Happy Dance

Princess Faith and Princess Charity are dancing and smiling because they are happy. They are glad to be outside on a beautiful day so they can enjoy God's creation.

God made the world for you to enjoy. He made pretty flowers and trees. He made furry bunnies to hop through the grass. He made birds to sing happy songs. If you enjoy all these things, then remember to tell God. You can thank him in your prayers and sing praises to let him know you enjoy his world.

Princess Faith's Prayer

Lord, I want to give you praise for many happy, joyful days.

Live Like a Daughter of the King

What do you enjoy most about God's creation? Be sure to thank God for the things you enjoy. You can even do a little happy dance!

*But may those who do what is right be glad
and filled with joy when they are with him.*
—*Psalm 68:3*

Enjoy Doing Good

Princess Joy and her sisters are happy to see their father return from his trip. They did some good things while he was away and they want to tell him all about it.

When you make a good decision or do something kind to help someone, it's fun to tell others what happened. You can tell your friends or people in your family. And you can thank God for giving you a chance to do something good. God is pleased when you enjoy doing good things.

Princess Joy's Prayer

Lord, it makes me feel so good whenever I do the things I should.

Live Like a Daughter of the King

It's hard to always do the right thing, but when you do, it's a great feeling. Ask God to help you do something good today, so you can enjoy the feeling.

Speak to one another with psalms, hymns and songs from the Spirit. Sing and make music from your heart to the Lord.
—*Ephesians 5:19*

Happy Hearts

The children that Princess Joy invited to her birthday party are so happy! They are filled with joy because they are in the castle celebrating with Joy and her sisters.

It's fun to celebrate someone's birthday, but you don't need to be at a birthday party to celebrate and be happy. God loves you so much that you can celebrate his love every day. You can sing praise songs and read your favorite Bible verses. Praising God will always put joy in your heart.

Princess Joy's Prayer

Your love is with me all day long! I'll praise you with a happy song.

Live Like a Daughter of the King

Do you have a favorite praise song that you like to sing or listen to? Before you go to bed tonight, use that song to praise God. Even if you've had a bad day, it can make you feel joyful.

The LORD has done great things for us. And we are filled with joy.
—Psalm 126:3

God is Good

The king and his daughters are saying good-bye to their new friends. They are happy that God was with Charity as she helped a boy from another kingdom.

God does great things for us every day. He takes care of us and blesses us with family and friends. He sends sunshine and rain to help the flowers grow. He gives us food to eat and water to drink. When you think of God's goodness and the way he cares for us, it's no wonder we can feel joyful!

Princess Charity's Prayer

Lord, you do great things for me, so I will praise you joyfully.

Live Like a Daughter of the King

Think about all the ways God takes care of you and blesses you. The more you can think of, the more joyful you will be!

A cheerful heart makes you healthy.
— Proverbs 17:22

Lots of Laughter

Princess Hope and Princess Faith are having a great time. Their joy is bubbling out of them and they can't stop laughing.

Did you know that laughing is good for you? God made our bodies so that laughter makes us feel better. It helps you forget about your problems and gives you more energy. When one person laughs, it usually makes other people laugh too. Soon everyone is smiling and laughing and feeling good inside. Laughter on the outside means joy on the inside.

Princess Hope's Prayer

Thank you for laughter
and smiles too.
Thank you for joy that
comes from you.

Live Like a Daughter of the King

Do you have a friend or someone in your family who makes you laugh? If you do, tell that person how much you like their happy and joyful spirit.

The LORD is great. He is really worthy of praise. Praise him in the city of our God, his holy mountain.
—Psalm 48:1

Praise Him

Princess Hope and her sisters are very excited! They are on their way to the kingdom's Easter celebration to remember the great sacrifice Jesus made for us on the cross.

Easter is a joyful time of year, but we can celebrate what Jesus did for us every day. Every day he loves us. Every day he forgives our sins. Every day he wants us to talk to him. You don't have to wait for Christmas or Easter to celebrate the love of Jesus. He loves you every day!

Princess Hope's Prayer

Lord Jesus,
I will celebrate.
I'll praise your name
for you are great.

Live Like a Daughter of the King

You can celebrate Jesus every day by talking to him when you pray and reading his stories in the Bible. And you can celebrate Jesus every day by telling him that you love him.

God is the King of the whole earth.
Sing a psalm of praise to him.
—Psalm 47:7

Praise and Sing

Princess Faith and Princess Hope are happy they are sisters. And they are happy that they are daughters of the king. They love to dance and sing in their beautiful yard by the bubbling fountain. They are praising God for the many blessings he gives them every day.

When you are happy on the inside, it shows on the outside. Knowing how much God loves you can make you happy inside. Being happy will put a smile on your face, and it might even make you dance and sing!

Princess Faith's Prayer

Lord, you are my God and King. I'll give you praises as I sing.

Live Like a Daughter of the King

Think of some ways you can praise God for being your King. Can you sing a song or write a poem? You can praise God with your words or with a song. God loves to hear your praises!

*The Lord is good to those who
put their hope in him.*
—*Lamentations 3:25*

Hoping for Good Things

Princess Joy hopes that she is a good sister. She hopes that she shows God's love to the people around her. And she hopes and prays that God has good plans for her when she grows up.

Did you know that God has wonderful plans for you because he loves you? You might not know all of his plans right away, but if you keep trusting and hoping and believing in God, he will show you his plans when the time is right.

Princess Joy's Prayer

*Help me, Lord, to
hope and pray,
so I will know your
plans someday.*

Live Like a Daughter of the King

What do you want to be when you grow up? You might change your mind a few times, but you can ask God to show you the good plans he has for you.

Commit to the LORD everything you do.
Then he will make your plans succeed.
—Proverbs 16:3

Making Plans

Princess Hope sees a beautiful ring that used to belong to her grandmother. She and her sisters will start making plans in hopes of getting the ring back.

When we make plans to do something, it's always important to ask God for his help and blessing. If what you want to do is something that will please God, then ask him to give you the wisdom and strength you need to get it done. When God is part of the plan, he will help you to be successful.

Princess Hope's Prayer

Bless me, Lord, and
bless my plans.
Guide me with your
loving hands.

Live Like a Daughter of the King

God is pleased when we make plans for something good. What kind of plans are you thinking about? Ask God to help you and let him be part of your plans.

He comforts us in all our troubles.
—2 Corinthians 1:4

No More Tears

Princess Joy is upset because she thinks her birthday party is going to be ruined. She cannot hold back her tears. The king is trying to comfort her. He tells her that everything will be fine.

It's okay to cry when you get upset—that's why God gave us tears! But God doesn't want you to stay upset forever. He wants you to talk to him and remember that he cares about you. God can comfort you and give you hope that things will get better.

Princess Joy's Prayer

Lord, comfort me
when I am sad.
Give me hope and
make me glad.

Live Like a Daughter of the King

No matter what kind of troubles you have, you can tell God and he will listen. Nothing is too big for God to handle. Let his love comfort you, give you hope, and wipe away your tears.

He has made everything beautiful in its time.
—Ecclesiastes 3:11

It Takes Time

Princess Faith is looking at her beautiful flower garden. She and her sisters worked hard planting the seeds and watering the soil. They remembered to pray and ask for God's help. Princess Faith was hoping the flowers would grow into something beautiful, and they did!

Just like it takes time for seeds to grow into beautiful flowers, it takes time for you to grow into the beautiful daughter God created you to be. The important thing is to trust God, be patient, and pray.

Princess Faith's Prayer

I'll trust you, Lord, because I know beautiful things take time to grow.

Live Like a Daughter of the King

It's easy to want to grow up too quickly. But every age is special and it's important to enjoy who you are right now. God will help you to keep growing and learning. It just takes time.

Find your delight in the LORD. Then he will give you
everything your heart really wants.
—Psalm 37:4

Please Say Yes!

Princess Grace cannot believe what she sees in the
closet! Five adorable kittens are looking right at her.
She wants to keep them, but she knows she needs to
ask the king. She is hoping he will say yes!

God is good and he wants you to have good things.
If you love God with all your heart, you will want the
same things that he wants for you. Ask God to fill your
heart with things that please him. Then you can ask him
for anything.

Princess Grace's Prayer

Fill my heart with
what is good,
so I will want the
things I should.

Live Like a Daughter of the King

Is there something that you are hoping for? Keep talking to God
about it and keep trusting him to do what is best. If what you
want is the same thing God wants for you, then the answer is yes.

With all my heart I wait for the LORD to help me.
I put my hope in his word.
—Psalm 130:5

Ask and Hope

Princess Hope knows there has to be a way to get her grandmother's ring back. As she thinks about what she can do, she believes in her heart that God will help her figure things out.

God wants to help you with whatever you need to do. Whether it's studying for an important test, or thinking of ways to help a friend, ask God to help you do your best. God cares about every part of your life, and he wants you to put your hope in him.

Princess Hope's Prayer

Lord, I know you
really care.
When I need help
you'll hear my prayer.

Live Like a Daughter of the King

What are three important things you want to do this week? Write them on a piece of paper and then pray about those things. Ask God to help you with everything you need to do.

The LORD is close to those whose
hearts have been broken.
—Psalm 34:18

God is Close

Princess Grace is very worried. One of her kittens is missing and she has no idea where it is. Grace is afraid something awful may have happened. She is hoping that her kitten will be found soon.

Sometimes bad things happen that make us start to worry. But when something bad happens, God wants you to talk to him right away. Tell God your concerns and ask him for his help. God is never far away—he's as close as a prayer!

Princess Grace's Prayer

Lord, I know you
are always close.
I can trust in
you the most.

Live Like a Daughter of the King

You might not always be with your parents or a close friend when something happens that worries you. But you are always close to God, and he is only a prayer away.

May the power of the Holy Spirit fill you with hope.
—Romans 15:13

Filled with Hope

Princess Hope is excited! She is hoping that she will find some hidden treasures behind the secret door. She is going to do whatever it takes to find out!

Did you know that hope is one of the gifts from the Holy Spirit? The hope that comes from the Holy Spirit is the kind of hope we have when we know God is in control. The Holy Spirit gives us hope that God will bless us and care for us. Receiving hope is like finding a hidden treasure!

Princess Hope's Prayer

Thank you, Lord,
for the hope you give.
I'll praise this gift
each day I live.

Live Like a Daughter of the King

If you are a daughter of the King, you can always have hope no matter what happens. If you are having troubles today, ask God to give you his love and power and fill you with hope.

LORD, in the morning you hear my voice.
In the morning I pray to you. I wait for you in hope.
—Psalm 5:3

Morning Prayers

Princess Joy is thankful for a new day. She is hoping today will be filled with God's blessings. She knows she can talk to God anytime, but she especially likes talking to God in the morning.

Talking to God in the morning is the best way to start your day. You can thank him for a new day and ask him to bless you and keep you safe. No matter if the morning is sunny or cloudy, or even pouring rain, start your day with a prayer and a smile!

Princess Joy's Prayer

Good morning, Lord.
Please bless my day.
I know you hear
me when I pray.

Live Like a Daughter of the King

What is the first thing you do in the morning? Do you eat breakfast or brush your teeth? Maybe you get dressed and make your bed. Remember to say a prayer in the morning. God loves to hear your morning voice!

*Put your hope in God. Once again I will have reason
to praise him. He is my Savior and my God.*
—Psalm 42:5

Hope and Praise

Princess Faith and her sisters are happy they were
able to help a little girl find her mother just before their
Easter celebration. They had prayed and asked God
to help them. God answered their prayers and kept
them safe. Now it was time to praise God and celebrate
Jesus.

There are many reasons to praise God. You can
praise him for answering your prayers. You can praise
him for Jesus. And you can praise him because he is a
God of hope.

Princess Faith's Prayer

*Lord, I'll put my
hope in you.
You're my God and
Savior too.*

Live Like a Daughter of the King

Think of four reasons why you can praise God. When you say
your prayers today, praise God for those reasons and thank him
for giving you hope.

*Grow in the grace and knowledge of our
Lord and Savior Jesus Christ.*
—2 Peter 3:18

Can't Earn It

Princess Faith enjoys reading books that help her learn more about God. She knows that the more she reads, the more she will understand how wonderful God is.

The Bible teaches us about God's grace. Grace means that God loves us so much he gives us blessings without us having to earn them. It's like getting an allowance even though you didn't do your chores. God doesn't want us to feel like we have to earn his love. He just wants us to love him and enjoy his grace.

Princess Faith's Prayer

*Lord, your grace is
awesome and free.
Thank you for the
grace you give to me.*

Live Like a Daughter of the King

Do you ever get an A on a test even though you got most of the answers wrong? Probably not! That's what it's like to have God's grace. You don't have to be perfect for God to give you his blessings. All you need to do is enjoy them!

So let us boldly approach God's throne of grace. Then we will receive mercy. We will find grace to help us when we need it.
—*Hebrews 4:16*

Talk to the King

Even though her father is an important king, Princess Joy is never afraid to talk to him. She has an idea that she wants to share with him, and she knows he is happy to listen to her.

God is more important than any other king, but you should never be afraid to tell him what's on your mind. God is kind and loving and full of grace. He is always happy to listen to your prayers and help you with whatever you need.

Princess Joy's Prayer

Thank you, Lord, for having time to hear what's on my heart and mind.

Live Like a Daughter of the King

Is there something you want to talk to God about, but you're not sure you should? God doesn't want you to be afraid. Whatever is on your mind—tell him today!

He heals those who have broken hearts.
He takes care of their wounds.
—Psalm 147:3

Sad Hearts

Princess Faith is sad because some of her flowers died. The king doesn't want her to be sad. He is trying to make her feel better by telling her she can try again.

Did you know that God doesn't want his children to be sad? But when they are, he will comfort them and help them feel better. Sadness is like a sore on the inside. God is good at healing inside sores. His love and grace can make his children feel like new!

Princess Faith's Prayer

Lord, when I am
sad and blue,
you can make me
feel like new.

Live Like a Daughter of the King

God cares if you are hurting on the inside, and he is good at making you feel better. Is there something you need to tell him today? If so, talk to him and let him heal your hurt.

Taste and see that the LORD is good. Blessed is
the person who goes to him for safety.
—Psalm 34:8

Really Good

Princess Joy thinks her birthday cake looks delicious! She can't wait to have a big slice so she can find out how good it really is.

The Bible says that God is good. But until we get to know God, we won't know how good he really is. You can get to know God by talking to him and reading the Bible. You can pray and ask him to help you with your problems. And when he answers your prayers, you will see how good he really is!

Princess Joy's Prayer

Lord, please help me
know and see
how good you
really are to me.

Live Like a Daughter of the King

Do you have a friend who you like to talk to? The more you talk to her, the better you know her. The same thing is true with God. Talk to him and get to know him better. He already knows all about you!

He has removed our sins from us. He has removed them
as far as the east is from the west.
—Psalm 103:12

Far Away

Princess Charity is looking out over the ocean. She is trying to see the land that's on the other side, but it is too far away.

When we tell God we are sorry for our sins, he forgives us. He takes our sins so far away it's like they are on the other side of the ocean. God doesn't see them anymore and he doesn't want us to see them either. Everyone sins and needs God's forgiveness. Because of his grace, he takes our sins far, far away.

Princess Charity's Prayer

Thank you, Lord,
that when I pray
you take my sins
so far away.

Live Like a Daughter of the King

Aren't you happy that God takes your sins far away? When you ask God to forgive your sins, you don't have to think about them anymore because they are gone for good!

Let the little children come to me. Don't keep them away.
God's kingdom belongs to people like them.
—Mark 10:14

Everyone Is Invited

Princess Joy invited the children of the kingdom to come to a party at the castle. They are celebrating with good food and lots of fun activities. Joy is going to give the children presents even though it's her birthday and not theirs!

That's what God's grace is like. He wants everyone to believe in him and become part of his family. He shares all his riches and blessings with us every day. He invites everyone into his kingdom—even children. God's kingdom belongs to everyone who believes in Jesus.

Princess Joy's Prayer

Your kingdom belongs
to everyone
who trusts in Jesus Christ
your Son.

Live Like a Daughter of the King

If you are a daughter of the King, then you belong to his kingdom. Do you know someone who doesn't know Jesus? Ask God to help you tell that person how to become a child of God.

But you are a God who forgives. You are gracious. You are tender and kind. You are slow to get angry. You are full of love.
—Nehemiah 9:17

A Little Mess

Princess Grace sees her kitten making a mess on the floor. Grace is not worried about her father being upset because she knows he is kind and forgiving. She knows he loves her no matter what. She will tell him she is sorry, and then she'll clean up the mess.

Sometimes our sins can seem like a mess. But you don't have to worry that God will be angry with you. If you believe in Jesus and are truly sorry for your sins, he will forgive you. He loves you no matter what.

Princess Grace's Prayer

Lord, you are kind and gracious too. I know forgiveness comes from you.

Live Like a Daughter of the King

Aren't you happy that God doesn't get angry with you because he loves you so much? Don't be afraid to tell him you are sorry when you mess up. He is kind and forgiving.

*The LORD is good to all. He shows deep
concern for everything he has made.*
—Psalm 145:9

Good to All

Princess Joy is happy that she is a daughter of
the king. But she is happy about other things too. She
is happy that her father and sisters care about her so
much. And she is happy that because of God's grace,
she has many blessings.

You probably don't live in a castle, and maybe
you don't have a lot of sisters. But you can be happy
because God's grace is for you too. He will shower you
with his love and blessings, because he cares about you
so much.

Princess Joy's Prayer

*Lord, I have a
happy face,
for you are good and
full of grace.*

Live Like a Daughter of the King

Think about something you enjoy that shows how much God
loves you. How can you show God that you love him?

May God our Father and the Lord Jesus Christ
give you grace and peace.
—2 Corinthians 1:2

Butterflies and Birds

Princess Charity is happy to be outdoors on a beautiful afternoon. She is smiling at the butterflies and listening to the birds sing their joyful songs.

It's easy to see how much God loves us when we can be outdoors and enjoy his creation. When we see how God cares for his creatures, we can know that he cares for us too. God cares for us because of his love and grace. We can have peace instead of worries, and we can enjoy butterflies and singing birds!

Princess Charity's Prayer

Thank you, Lord,
for butterflies,
for singing birds,
and sunny skies.

Live Like a Daughter of the King

What kind of creatures do you see when you go outdoors? How does God care for them? How does God care for you?

God's grace has saved you because of your faith in Christ.
Your salvation doesn't come from anything you do. It is God's gift.
—Ephesians 2:8

The Greatest Grace

Princess Hope and her sisters love their Easter celebration each year. They enjoy meeting people from other lands who join them in singing praises and listening to the story of Jesus as they gather at the cross.

Jesus died on the cross so we can be forgiven of our sins. When we believe in Jesus as our Savior, God gives us the gift of salvation. We cannot earn our salvation. It is a gift to us from God because of his wonderful grace.

Princess Hope's Prayer

Lord, your grace is
great and true.
Salvation is a
gift from you.

Live Like a Daughter of the King

What are some good gifts you have received from your family? Even your favorite gift cannot compare with God's gift of salvation. When you say your prayers tonight, thank God for his grace and for the gift of salvation.

Faith is being sure of what we hope for.
It is being sure of what we do not see.
—*Hebrews 11:1*

It's for Real

Princess Hope and her sisters are blessed to live in a castle. They enjoy having beautiful things because they are daughters of the king.

Most people do not live in castles or fancy homes. But someday they can. God has a beautiful mansion in heaven where we can live someday if we believe in Jesus. Having faith means you believe in something even though you can't see it. We can't see Jesus, and we can't see God's mansion, but we know they are real because the Bible says so.

Princess Hope's Prayer

Someday, Lord,
your face I'll see
because I know
you died for me.

Live Like a Daughter of the King

Can you imagine what it would be like to live in a castle? The Bible tells us that God's home in heaven is more beautiful than anything we can imagine. You can enjoy your home on earth and look forward to your home in heaven!

*God began a good work in you. And I am sure that
he will carry it on until it is completed.*
—Philippians 1:6

More to Come

Princess Faith is thinking about the blessings she enjoys like books and bunnies and sisters. But she knows there are more blessings to come. As she grows older, God will continue to bless her and show her the plans he has for her.

If you are a daughter of the King, you can have faith that God will bless you and guide you throughout your life. You can believe that God has good plans for you. And even in hard times, God will be with you every step of the way.

Princess Faith's Prayer

*Thank you that
you'll always stay
right beside me
all the way.*

Live Like a Daughter of the King

Isn't it exciting to know that you have so much to look forward to? God created you because he wants you to be here. You can believe that he will stay with you for your whole life!

Don't let anyone look down on you
because you are young.
—1 Timothy 4:12

Not Too Young

Princess Charity is the youngest princess in her family, but she is fearless and adventurous. She is telling the king how she got into a scary situation that required her to be brave and take action.

Even though you are young, you are important. God loves it when you stand up for what is right or lend a hand when someone needs help. He loves it when you show others what it means to be a Christian by the way you live. With God, you are never too young!

Princess Charity's Prayer

Lord, I may be
young and small,
but I'll have faith to
stand up tall!

Live Like a Daughter of the King

Sometimes it seems like children have more faith than adults. It doesn't matter to God how old you are. What matters is that you believe in him, trust him, and love him.

The LORD will keep all his promises.
He is faithful in everything he does.
—Psalm 145:13

God Is Faithful

Princess Hope loves picking flowers from the bushes in her yard. She knows the flowers will bloom every spring and be beautiful.

Just like we can count on springtime flowers to bloom every year, we can count on God to keep his promises to us. God promises to bless you and keep you in his care. He promises to love you no matter what. God is faithful in keeping his promises to you, and he wants you to be faithful in trusting him.

Princess Hope's Prayer

Lord, you are faithful in everything— like flowers blooming in the spring.

Live Like a Daughter of the King

Have you ever made a promise that was hard to keep? God has no problem keeping his promises. The Bible is full of God's promises, and he keeps each one.

His great love is new every morning.
LORD how faithful you are!
—Lamentations 3:23

Love in the Morning

Princess Charity loves saying good morning to Daisy. Every morning, Charity visits Daisy to make sure she is okay. Charity is faithful in caring for Daisy, because she loves her.

When you get up in the morning, you can think about how much God loves you. The Bible says God is faithful and his love is new every morning. You can be faithful in your love for God too. He never gets tired of hearing you say, "I love you." Tell God you love him— morning, noon, or night.

Princess Charity's Prayer

Morning, noon,
and nighttime too,
I will tell you,
"I love you!"

Live Like a Daughter of the King

Think of three different times today when you can tell God you love him. That's one of the ways that you can be faithful to God!

*Be still, and know that I am God. I will be honored
among the nations. I will be honored in the earth.*
—*Psalm 46:10*

Be Still

As Princess Faith walks around outside of the
castle, she is amazed by all the beauty she sees. She
is going to be still and enjoy God's creation.

Sometimes it's good to be still so you can enjoy
the things God has made. You can watch clouds travel
through the sky or listen to quacking ducks. You can
look at leaves blowing in the wind or watch a ladybug
crawl over a flower. When you see the things that only
God can create, you know he is real.

Princess Faith's Prayer

*Lord, you make the
leaves to blow,
and you can make
the flowers grow.*

Live Like a Daughter of the King

The next time you have a chance to be outside, sit still for a while.
Listen for animal sounds and see if you can tell what kind of animal
is making the noises. Count how many things you see that God
made. After a while, you will feel like God is right next to you!

Trust in the LORD with all your heart. Do not depend on your own understanding.
—*Proverbs 3:5*

Depend on God

The princesses are on an adventure and they are not sure how things are going to turn out. They are trusting God to help them even though they don't understand all the details.

When you trust in God, it means you depend on him. It means you know he will guide you and help you understand what he wants you to do. You don't have to know everything that will happen tomorrow or the next day. Just ask God to help you understand his plans for today.

Princess Grace's Prayer

Lord, I'll trust you every day. Lead me, guide me all the way.

Live Like a Daughter of the King

Aren't you happy that you don't have to understand what's going to happen in the days ahead? God knows everything about your future. All you need to do is let him lead the way!

*Be on your guard. Remain
strong in the faith. Be brave.*
—*1 Corinthians 16:13*

Princess Prayer

Princess Faith and her sisters are enjoying some tea as they travel through the forest. The sky is getting dark and it looks like rain. Their faith in God will help them be strong as they face the storm.

Whenever you are afraid of something that might happen, ask God to protect you and keep you safe. God will listen to you and help you. Your faith in God will keep you strong to make it through the hard times. And when it's over—your faith will be even stronger!

Princess Faith's Prayer

*Give me faith that's
always strong,
for you are with me
all day long.*

Live Like a Daughter of the King

Is there something that you are worrying about? God doesn't want you to worry. He wants you to put your faith in him and let him take care of things. Ask him to help you trust him with everything.

Jesus Christ is the same yesterday and today and forever.
—Hebrews 13:8

Always the Same

The king and his five princess daughters enjoy the flowers and trees in their yard. They always look forward to summer when everything is fresh and green. Summer comes after the spring season and spring comes after winter. Every year, it's always the same, and that will never change.

The Bible says that Jesus will never change. He is always the same—every day and every season of the year. That means his promises will never change, and his love for you will always be the same.

Princess Joy's Prayer

Jesus, I will trust
your name,
for you will always
stay the same.

Live Like a Daughter of the King

Think about the things in your life that keep changing. Your age changes every year. Your friends change. Maybe you've even changed where you live. When things around you keep changing, remember that Jesus will never change, and he will always love you.

Not even the highest places or the lowest, or anything else in all creation can separate us. Nothing at all can ever separate us from God's love.
—Romans 8:39

Wherever You Go

Princess Hope knows that her father loves her very much. She knows that no matter where she goes, and no matter what she does, he will always love her.

The Bible tells us that nothing can separate us from God's love. No matter where you go or what you do, God will never stop loving you. You can go up the highest mountain or swim deep in the sea, and God's love will follow you. God promises to love you—always and forever.

Princess Hope's Prayer

I love you, Lord,
with all my heart.
Nothing on earth
can keep us apart.

Live Like a Daughter of the King

No matter what happens in your life, God will never stop loving you. You can never lose his love or have it taken away. How can you say "thank you" to God for his never ending love?

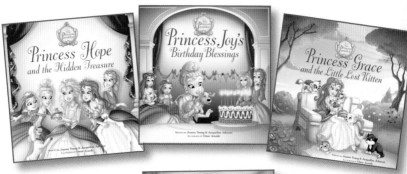

ZONDERkidz

I Can Read! 1
BEGINNING READING

ZONDERkidz I Can Read! 1

Princess Grace
and Poppy

Story inspired by Jeanna Young & Jacqueline Johnson
Pictures by Omar Aranda

ZONDERkidz I Can Read! 1

Princess Faith's
Garden Surprise

Story inspired by Jeanna Young & Jacqueline Johnson
Pictures by Omar Aranda

ZONDERkidz I Can Read! 1

Princess Joy's
Party

Story inspired by Jeanna Young & Jacqueline Johnson
Pictures by Omar Aranda

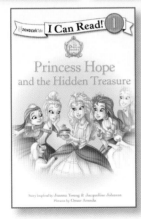

ZONDERkidz I Can Read! 1

Princess Hope
and the Hidden Treasure

Story inspired by Jeanna Young & Jacqueline Johnson
Pictures by Omar Aranda

ZONDERkidz I Can Read! 1

Princess Charity's
Golden Heart

Story inspired by Jeanna Young & Jacqueline Johnson
Pictures by Omar Aranda

Also available

STICKER BOOKS

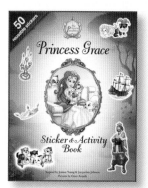

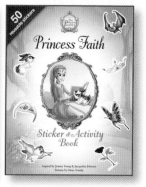